Teach The Geek To Speak

Neil Thompson

ISBN-13: 978-0578410111
ISBN-10: 0578410117

Library of Congress Cataloging-in-Publication Date is available.

Legal Disclaimer

While none of the stories in this book are fabricated, some of the names and details may have been changed to protect the privacy of the individuals mentioned. Although the author and publisher have made every effort to ensure that the information in this book was correct at press time, the author and publisher do not assume and hereby disclaim any liability to any party for any loss, damage, or disruption caused by errors or omissions, whether such errors or omissions result from negligence, accident, or any other cause.

Ordering Information

Teach the Geek to Speak may be purchased in large quantities at a discount for educational, business, or sales promotional use. For information email:

Request Mr. Neil Thompson

Email: hello@teachthegeek.com

Dedication

To my nephew, Anthony, who is a special boy.
I'm certain you will grow to be a special man.

Public speaking is someone else's job
. . . until it's yours.

~ Neil Thompson

Contents

Introduction

Are you a STEM professional like me? If you are, and frankly even if you are not, you will likely agree that public speaking is *not* the strong suit of most geeks. If you are anything like I was, it's not your strong suit either. I know for certain that while my peers and I were thriving at physics, chemistry, and calculus, it came to a painfully screeching halt when we were asked to speak publicly to anyone about anything. Nonetheless, as I soon learned, STEM professionals who want to excel in their careers and become true assets to their companies absolutely must learn how to give effective presentations.

Therefore, if our paths have crossed because you are also a STEM professional who has realized this, I designed the *Teach the Geek to Speak* process, wrote the book and the accompanying workbook, and created the online course especially for you!

In the straightforward, concise, and logical manner that most STEM types appreciate, *Teach the Geek to Speak* explains to you precisely how to deal with why you are shying away from public speaking. It offers you a process to help you to understand the steps to get your mind right, develop yourself personally and professionally, and learn how to prepare your speech from beginning to end. I even tell you what you should do *after* you speak to make a lasting impression on your audience.

I decided to stop working so that I could speak, teach, and train STEM professionals nationally. Prior to doing this, I was a Product Development Engineer in the medical device industry. In that role, I was looking for the path to promotion within my company. When I found that the key skill to get on the fast track to success was the ability to speak well, I committed to learning everything I could about public speaking. I invested my money and my time into becoming an excellent speaker by reading, taking classes, and speaking more at work and in other venues. As a result, my public speaking improved dramatically, and my bosses began to notice. I was appointed to leadership roles at work and received several promotions.

However, in my quest to master public speaking, I found that most available training lacked a clear process to follow.

I knew that if my colleagues were to also benefit, they would need training and teaching that included a process that other STEM professionals could easily follow.

I could not find that process, so I created it.

My goal with *Teach the Geek to Speak* is to provide you with an effective and efficient way to give any speech. The *Teach the Geek to Speak* process is an easy to follow and streamlined six-step process that any STEM processional can understand and use immediately. This process is designed to be applicable to any type of speech that you need to give. Therefore, whether you have been assigned to give a project status update, conference talk, webinar presentation, teach a class on your area of expertise, or anything else, you will be prepared. You can rest assured that, with the *Teach the Geek to Speak* process, you will be able to give a stellar presentation.

The course (which includes the book and supplementary materials) is intended for STEM professionals like you. While I was not satisfied with my status in my company, learning to speak well helped me to improve personally, professionally, and financially.

As we work through these five chapters together, you will be challenged to reflect and practice skills that may initially seem foreign or uncomfortable to you. However, if you stick with the process, you will see, like I did, that you'll become more knowledgeable about how to present. Your audience will no longer play on their cell phones or zone out during your talks. Even when they do not necessarily understand all the technical terms in your talk, you will become skilled at presenting without using fillers or relying entirely on your notes. You will learn how to use visualization and several other proven, research-based techniques so you will stop feeling so fearful or disorganized when you are asked to speak.

So, let's get started!

The Making of Neil Thompson: The Geek Who Speaks

Chapter 1

Nothing in life is to be feared, it is only to be understood. Now is the time to understand more, so that we may fear less.

~ Marie Curie

I am the only boy in my family. I am the middle child who is wedged between two sisters. I was reared by two loving parents, who were determined that my sisters and I would become the very best people and professionals possible. My parents had very high expectations for all of us. While it may be normal for the middle kid to get lost in the shuffle, the exact opposite was true for me.

My beautiful, loving, and doting mother shone her spotlight on me. I often resented what I felt as a young child was the extra attention she constantly paid to me. One of the things that really bothered me was that she wouldn't stop pushing me onto the stage. It seemed like my mother was always looking for an opportunity for me to speak in public.

Both of my parents are immigrants. My mother is from Grenada, while my father is from Trinidad. I emigrated from Canada to the United States in 2002 to attend university.

My mother raised us in the Roman Catholic Church. We grew up faithfully attending services in a loving Catholic community that was filled with joyful, kind, driven people who, like my parents, wanted the best for themselves and their children. Our church was like a second home, where we learned, ate, laughed, and celebrated our culture and faith together. There was rarely a time when I was not performing, or preparing to perform, in some special presentation. In these programs and services (all of which my mother volunteered me for), I would speak before the congregation. Over the years, I performed in many church plays (mostly during

Christmas), and I had to read scripture and many other things before the congregation.

My mother's mission was to ensure that I was involved in church and developed into a well-rounded man and well-spoken individual. I was definitely not forgotten about as the middle child and the only boy. My mom made sure that I was the leader or that I had a starring role in almost everything that required speaking before a crowd. I therefore overcame my fear of speaking at a very young age. This did not occur because I loved the stage and wanted to be involved with public speaking. It was due to my mother's insistence that I participate. Like most children I knew during this era, I did as I was told.

As a result, starting when I was just nine years old, I was not afraid to speak in public. However, I never loved it. Therefore, when I turned 18 years old and started to attend university, I abandoned public speaking entirely. My mother was no longer there to force me to do things, including public speaking. Therefore, for over four years, I did not speak publicly at all.

I was able to avoid public speaking in both college and graduate school. Since my first job after graduate school was working in a lab, I even avoided public speaking after entering the workforce. In fact, one of the best parts of being a Lab Associate for two years was that I never had to do work presentations.

I came to California in late 2007 when I accepted a job as a Product Development Engineer at a medical device company. I loved that my new job in Southern California allowed me to go outside in my shorts and a hat and to ditch my ice scraper! However, there was one vital aspect of my new position that I did not love. Every month I had to make a presentation before the CEO and other senior managers. Unlike the other companies where I was employed, this new company did not hire Project Managers. Instead, they relied upon their Product Development Engineers to serve as Project Leads. This meant that I needed to handle many activities in addition to my primary duties.

I did not know that this was required by the company when I accepted the position. If I had been aware of this responsibility, I would have never accepted the job. Although my mother had prepared me for public speaking, I had managed to avoid this task so far in my career.

Now that I was in this position and since my mother had prepared me to do this, I knew exactly what I needed to do to meet this challenge.

Although my mother had prepared me for public speaking, I had not spoken publicly for many years and I was very rusty. However, I was young and much cockier than was reasonable in this situation. I thought that my old poetry reading and scripture recitation skills had prepared me for these talks, and I decided to wing it.

That first presentation did not go well.

When I entered the room, at least twenty stoic-faced senior managers were sitting there, waiting to hear what I had to say. It became immediately apparent that I was not merely presenting poetry in a church service. This was a big deal and I was shaking like a leaf. My mouth was as dry as a Brillo pad. To make matters worse, I was sweating so profusely that any onlooker would have thought that I had just emerged from a hot, steamy shower. I was stumbling over my words and there was no one there to save me. Sometimes, we can rescue a presentation that is going poorly. However, this presentation was not salvageable. I did not have to wait until the end of the presentation to know that I had totally bombed the talk. The question-and-answer session was even worse than the presentation itself.

The executives looked perplexed as to how I had been assigned the lead on anything. My team's faces showed their lack of confidence in my ability to lead the project. I was thoroughly embarrassed and in desperate need of a shower to wash away my sweat and my shame.

I knew that I could not go on presenting this way. I was extremely stressed out and humiliated. I had blown this important presentation. However, I was fortunate that I had been humbled. This is because that day was the start of what has become the hallmark of my passion and life's work -- to help other STEM professionals prepare themselves to manage their fear of public speaking and to present effectively. In that boardroom on that unforgettable day, Teach the Geek to Speak was born.

The Last Straw

I used to work at a company that was started by a former boss of mine. I'd worked with him for about a year until he left the company. I really liked working for this guy. However, he left our company and started his own business. After he started his company, I asked him if I could work for him. I was the third employee at the startup. I enjoyed working there for many reasons. I was working with people that I liked in my area of expertise. I also lived close to my job, so I could walk to work every day. I just loved it.

My boss, however, eventually moved the company. When he relocated my job, I moved again so that I could avoid a long commute to work. I worked at that organization for about four more years. After three and a half years, I grew restless with my assignments. I wanted and asked for new challenges and suggested ways in which I could help contribute to the company's bottom line. However, for some reason, my boss ignored my requests to do more than what I was doing.

In April 2014, my boss, who was Indian, and his wife, who was White, adopted a little Black girl. I was inspired by their willingness to open their home to a child in need. I was happy for their family. I bought them books about adoption and a lovely Black baby doll for their daughter. Both he and his wife seemed to appreciate my gesture. One day I came across an article about the issues that families who chose adoption have with Black children's hair. I am Black. I lived with and love my Black mother and both of my Black sisters. I understand that, as gorgeous as it is, Black people's hair requires a particular method of care if it is to look its very best. Intrigued by the article and continuing my pattern of showing interest and celebrating that my boss and his wife had adopted a little girl in need, I thought, "Wow, this is useful information that will help my boss, his wife and their precious daughter. I should share this article with them." I watched my mother comb through my sisters' hair and knew that it could be painful if not done with the proper technique and tender loving care. I knew that their little daughter would benefit from my sharing the information. They had received my gifts with appreciation in the past, so I thought that they would also be appreciative of this gesture. However, that wasn't the case.

My boss blasted me with an angry email that said something like, "I wish you'd put as much effort into your work as you did into sending me this article." I was confused and stunned. I was so taken aback that I read the email several times, just to be sure that I had not misread it. It said exactly what I'd first read. "Put more effort into my work," I huffed. I was a disgruntled but model employee. This response was unwarranted and unfair. It was also exactly what I needed to push me over the edge. I now realize that it was a critical step I needed to take so that I could realize my greater destiny.

Until that day, I had never left a job without giving two-week's notice. I am a very deliberate and stable person. I do not tend to make decisions hastily. However, his response to what I thought was a kind deed caused me to act totally out of character.

I replied to his email, "I am sorry that I sent you the article. I thought it would be helpful. I did not mean to offend you and your wife. I had no idea that you were so unhappy with my work, so effective immediately--I quit!" I clicked send, placed my work phone on the desk, and left.

About seven months later, another medical device company hired me as an independent contractor. I worked in the office with other employees and enjoyed my work there. One day, I was abruptly let go, without warning due to no fault of my own. They gave me the infamous, "We're just going another direction," as their parting words.

That was the last straw. I was frustrated and angry beyond words and in that moment, I promised myself, "This is the first and last time that I will ever allow a CEO to call me into the office to tell me they're done with me." That was where my penchant for entrepreneurship truly began. I have worked for myself ever since.

Mindset Matters

Chapter 2

You cannot teach a man anything; you can only help him discover it in himself.

~ Galileo

Begin with Personal Discovery. One of the most vital challenges to embrace, when embarking on a process of personal discovery, is the fact that, along the way, you will discover things about yourself that you don't like.

I know this firsthand because I have often become so flustered by the mistakes I was making as a speaker that I completely missed the true goal of public speaking.

As exemplified by my epic failure in my first presentation to the senior management team, what really caused me to fail is that I entered the process of preparing with the wrong mindset. Thankfully, I quickly realized that my mindset needed to change. I had an epiphany. That awakening was the impetus that moved me to take the actions necessary to learn how to prepare, present, close, and follow up after my presentations. This allowed me to get my managers, my team, and I the results that I wanted. Whatever your previous speaking experiences are, you can make adjustments that will improve your competence and confidence and cause you to feel like a rock star every time you drop the mic.

I am not sure how you would rate yourself as a speaker. However, I had become so unaccustomed to presenting that my primary goal was simply to get through my talk without huge sweat stains on my dress shirt. Imagine someone who is standing before a room of his superiors and colleagues while sweating profusely in the process of trying to get through a truly lousy presentation. That was me. I was the sweaty, stumbling, and unprepared engineer, going through an awful slide deck while clicking my heels. I had the dubious hope that with one of the clicks, the sweat would miraculously dry. I wanted to be beamed from the boardroom until I could figure out how to get my mind right and be given another chance to give this presentation.

In STEM (science, technology, engineering and math) fields, there are reasons for scientists and engineers to need to speak publicly. These reasons include the desire to gain more visibility within the company, to improve their status within the company or within the field at large, to earn a pay increase, and to be selected to travel and speak on behalf of the company at national or international conferences. A Columbia University study found that people who are afraid to speak in public earn ten percent less than their peers who learn to conquer this fear.

I have personal experience with the professional benefits of overcoming my initial dread of speaking about my work. I had the honor of presenting my research at the 2013 International Combined Orthopedic Research Society conference in Venice, Italy. Several months before the event, my colleagues and I decided to submit our application with an abstract for consideration. If we were selected, our research would be featured at the conference. Several months before the conference, the Research Society's committee reviewed the applications to decide which authors to invite. Those who were selected to be invited could be asked to give a poster presentation, oral presentation, or both. Most of the applicants wanted to be chosen to give an oral presentation. Although I would have been happy with just the poster presentation, my colleagues and I were invited to speak from the stage. To make the invitation even more exciting, I had never been to Europe. I was quite thrilled about the entire situation.

Why even apply to present publicly? We wanted to gain more clout within the scientific community for the product that we had developed. We knew that we would be speaking to an audience of students, scholars, scientists and other professionals. We needed to expose our product and our findings to those attending that conference. We also understood that by presenting at a science-based rather than an industry-based conference, our company and our message would stand out. Thankfully, we were able to achieve all our goals. Not only did I get to enjoy a phenomenal trip to Italy and eat the most delicious, authentic pizza ever, but after that presentation, we were able to advertise in our company's marketing collateral, and on our individual resumes, that we were international conference presenters at a science-based conference. This greatly increased our credibility among both scientific and industry leaders.

It is crucial to recognize the numerous benefits of learning to present effectively. It is also important to look for opportunities to share your work with the audiences who will benefit by hearing from you. When you do this, you will find, like I did, that there are many fantastic opportunities for professionals who speak about their work. These opportunities are not available to professionals who don't speak about their work. Let's look at some of the factors that cause STEM professionals to hesitate to speak in public.

I have found that the three things holding STEM professionals back from public speaking are: the excuse factor, the fear factor and the belief factor.

The Excuse Factor

I've often made what I thought were perfectly valid excuses for not investing the time and taking the responsibility for preparing and presenting anything more than the crappy presentations that I decided to put together. "Does this sound familiar?" My excuses ranged from the classic, "I needed more time to prepare," to "Ah, my mom used to make me do this so much as a child that I am ruined! Public speaking is just not for me." I even went as far as to tell everyone that I'd practiced my speech for weeks and that I had no idea why "I froze once I was on stage."

The truth is that despite my excuses, whether they were true or lies, I had to improve. This was because my less than stellar presentations had put me on the back burner at my employers. It had prevented me from getting on the fast track to moving up the corporate ladder.

Facing these hard truths was a major step forward for me in my personal discovery process. Once I changed my mindset and decided to improve, I began to get the results that I wanted. By giving terrible presentations, it left me feeling like I imagine Michael Jordan must have felt when he was not selected to play varsity basketball during his sophomore year of high school. However, instead of wallowing in my failure, I did what great people do--I kept trying. Michael Jordan was rejected and could not play varsity with the senior basketball players, but he did not give up. He played basketball on the junior varsity team until the following year. Then he crushed it! As a matter of fact, he went on to play for the University of North Carolina, winning a championship while there. With the Chicago Bulls in the NBA, he won six championships. Michael Jordan is currently a billionaire who owns a professional basketball team in the NBA. He left his excuses at the door. I also stopped making excuses for myself. I began to work harder at perfecting my preparation and presentation skills. When I did this, the game totally changed for me. Change your mindset. Identify and reject all your excuses and watch the game change in your favor, too.

The Fear Factor
The second most limiting factor relating to public speaking for STEM professionals is the fear factor. We make some

of the excuses because we are just too lazy to prepare and to practice the craft of speaking well. STEM professionals can also be unaware of how being an excellent presenter can positively impact their careers. We often make excuses because we are just afraid to stand before a crowd to say anything.

It is true that STEM professionals are often introverts. Introverts are not necessarily shy people. However, they prefer solace over social stimulation or a quiet brunch with one friend instead of a wild and crazy party with many friends. This is perfectly fine. Of course, not all people in the STEM fields are introverts. However, the STEM professionals are in excellent company, because, as Gareth Cook acknowledges in an article entitled, *The Power of Introverts: A Manifesto for Quiet Brilliance*, "From Darwin to Picasso to Dr. Seuss, our greatest thinkers have often worked in solitude." If you happen to be in this field and you are much more comfortable behind the scenes than with a microphone in your hand, it's okay. Glossophobia, also known as speech anxiety or the fear of speaking, is recognized in the medical field as an actual social anxiety disorder. However, as the thousands of people who have taken the *Teach the Geek to Speak* course have learned, the fear factor can be addressed. With a proven process, you can become an effective public speaker.

You need a strategic action plan. By addressing the fear, a little at a time, you'll eventually conquer it. Let's face what we fear, because even if your audience can't see you sweating profusely through your clothing like I did, they can sense when you are afraid. You want to avoid this because, if they sense your fear, it makes you seem less credible and also makes them uncomfortable. When I first began to present on a professional level, I was terrified of receiving questions from audience members that I could not answer. This was one of my greatest fears. However, I faced it exactly how United States Army General Creighton Adams advised his troops to handle circumstances that seem insurmountable, when he said, "When eating an elephant, take one bite at a time."

When it comes to presenting, what are you most afraid of? Make a list, then tackle each item one fear at a time, until you learn to successfully work past all of them. It is important you understand that the fear may not go away completely. I still cope with my fears by taking deep breaths and counting to ten. I also boost my energy and esteem by reciting positive affirmations. Taking small, intentional, and strategic steps every day will enable you to manage the fear factor and accomplish your goals.

The Belief Factor

Once you address the fear factor, the second factor that keeps STEM professionals from polishing their speaking skills is belief.

Once you acknowledge and dismiss your excuses and confront your fears, you must start to believe that you can accomplish what you set your mind to. You have to believe that you will get what you are working to attain. While your mindset is key, I want to focus on how belief in yourself can be fostered when you pause and plan. STEM professionals are very strategic. We follow systems and formulas and we plan. This is another reason I show the professionals I coach how to follow a process that teaches them to speak. The process enables STEM professionals who want to become better speakers to reflect, write, and create action items with milestones. This will help them to clarify what they want to happen as a result of improving their speaking skills. The process also helps to measure your progress toward the goal.

I believed that I could become a better speaker. However, I also understood that I had to become a better speaker. I came to realize that was the only way I was going to excel in my profession.

As I described earlier, I was not doing well with presenting at work. However, instead of focusing solely on my poor presentation skills, I decided to celebrate what I could do well and to become laser focused on presenting like a pro. With time and practice, I eventually improved because I consistently worked on it. I had an outline with measurable goals and the action steps to make the goals a reality. I invested in learning to become an effective speaker because I believed that I could become one.

Mindset Matters

I have come a long way from my days of gigantic sweat stains as large as my head on my shirt. My growth occurred in part because I worked on my speaking skills. However, I also grew because I worked on my mindset and embraced my personal discovery journey. You will also need to do this.

As world-renowned public speaker Lisa Nichols often says, we must trust ourselves and the divine in us and believe that everything works together to support us living our best life.

You have to trust that no matter how much work you have to do to sharpen your saw, when it comes to improving as a STEM speaker, once you do the work, the rest will take care of itself. Learning to speak well, like many things, is related to your mindset.

In many of the STEM professions, we frequently use the prefixes micro and macro. These prefixes are also important in the context of speaking effectively. Once you outline your reasons for improving as a speaker and your plan for when and how you will meet certain milestones, there is still other planning that needs to take place. Researchers claim that we become 42 percent more likely to achieve our goals by simply writing them down regularly. Yes, you also need to plan for each time you are going to speak.

I remember how nervous I would become before making a presentation to management or an audience of my peers. It is not easy to communicate technical information with passion and in a way that gets the audience to care about what you are saying to them. However, as you practice the strategies and process that I share with you in *Teach the Geek to Speak*, you will improve and you will start to meet your goals. These wins -- small and big – are important to recognize and to celebrate.

Top professional speakers and trainers teach about the importance, when you decide to engage in the struggle to learn something new, of celebrating both your micro-wins and your macro-wins. Micro-wins lead to macro-wins. Sometimes, the macro-wins, which are the larger goals that we are striving toward, can seem to be out of reach. This is because micro-wins are easier and can be accomplished faster. You have an overarching outline and individual outlines and goals for each talk you need to give. After all, you want to get noticed more at work, considered for a promotion, selected to travel nationally or abroad on behalf of your company, or accomplish your personal and professional goals. That is key. However, as I learned in my process, improving as a speaker is a marathon. It is not a sprint. You will benefit most when you are patient and flexible and when you celebrate all your wins – both micro and macro.

As the saying goes, Rome wasn't built in a day. Similarly, your speaking skills will not be built overnight. You should first decide why you need to polish these skills. The next step is to outline your plan for becoming an effective speaker. You should also outline your presentations to your teams, managers, clients, and larger audiences. This strategy helps you to develop a healthy mindset about this process and increases your confidence, one presentation at a time. Mindset matters.

Commit to Your Success
In order to perfect the skill of speaking in ways that specifically benefit you as a STEM professional, you must commit to your success. Being able to commit in the ways that eventually bring you the success you want and deserve in your field is the result of developing an, "All I

do is win!" mindset. By the time I finish my personal empowerment routine, my mindset is in great shape. You should develop your own special personal rituals to pump yourself up and to establish the right mindset.

I began to more consistently speak about the experiments that I was working on because I'd come to realize what many STEM professionals fail to acknowledge. I realized that for me to excel, I *had* to be effective in sharing my expertise with STEM professionals and professionals in other industries. I realized that if I could articulate what I had done behind the scenes to both scientists and non-scientists, I would significantly increase my value to my employers and to the people who were affected by my work. I finally learned that what I said to others about by experiments was just as important as conducting the experiments.

I also began to see what I want to help you see. I could have everything I wanted because I was finally willing to release my limiting beliefs. As logical as it seems, when you decide that you want to learn to speak more effectively, you have to give up the belief that you can't become an effective speaker.

World renowned best-selling author, speaker, and psychologist Dr. Robert Anthony has over thirty years of experience studying mind power development. In Dr.

Anthony's words, "You can have anything you want, as long as you are willing to give up the belief that you can't have it."

For example, I decided that I needed to expand my horizons and emerge from quietly working in my cubicle. I decided that I wanted to get on the radar of senior management. To do this, I had to get in front of people who would listen to what I had to say. I had to commit to do the work it would take to improve myself and to earn the professional status and pay that I deserved. I especially had to commit to honing my skills once I decided that I wanted to become a paid professional speaker.

Being committed is not about how you feel. It is about having the audacity and drive to do the work it takes to reach the finish line. I simply gave myself the permission to do the work and I got it done. I literally wrote a list, referred to the list often, stared at the words, internalized them, and ultimately actualized them. I became successful because I was sick and tired of repeatedly giving in to my fears. I set my intentions, made a commitment to myself, and forged ahead. I also gave myself the time and space to win.

Committing to success includes practicing your public speaking skills in one setting and then becoming skilled at how to use those skills in other industries, settings or situations; using them gives you the opportunity to excel.

An excellent example of an individual who used his skills in one arena to gain entry and achieve success in other fields is LL Cool J (Ladies Love Cool James), a hip-hop artist and actor, who brilliantly succeeded at sharing his gifts across platforms. Traditionally, someone like LL Cool J would only operate within the realm of the hip-hop industry. However, over the last few decades, he has grown from having a small role in the cult hip-hop classic, *Krush Groove*, to having his own sitcom in the late 1990s called "In the House." We now see him on "NCIS: Los Angeles" and "Lip Sync Battle." Eventually, he transitioned his skills to movies and film and hosted award shows, such as the Annual Grammy Awards from 2012 to 2016. He strategically expanded his brand in the entertainment world by dominating radio (he released 13 albums and 2 compilation greatest hits albums), acting, and entrepreneurship (he has his own fashion lines), as well as being a husband and father.

We are STEM professionals. However, LL Cool J's story serves as an excellent case study of how, with the proper mindset and commitment, we can transcend our current roles in STEM. His story demonstrates what can happen when we sharpen our skills, recreate our vision for ourselves, and expand our influence by working both within and outside our normal spheres of influence. This is how I successfully combined being an engineer with becoming a public speaker who now teaches other STEM professionals to speak.

Committing to success requires you to set goals with deadlines. You want to ensure that your goals are clear. You should know when you want to achieve them and have a roadmap for meeting those deadlines. Committing to success means that you will begin to identify the people who are doing what you imagine yourself doing. Once you do this, you can schedule time to listen to, learn from, and be around those people. You should intentionally create professional circles in which you will be challenged. To become better (in your field or as a speaker), you need to decide to step outside your comfort zone.

Finally, my commitment to read more made a notable impact on my ability to speak well. Reading helps to keep us sharp and relevant in our fields. By reading more in a variety of areas, we can close the gaps in understanding and applying different concepts. If you let the experts in books, magazines, and articles become your mentors and teachers, you will shorten your learning curve.

It is important to remember that becoming a great speaker takes time. The journey is much more enjoyable if you map out your journey, gather what you need for the trip, and exercise patience during the ride.

While the proper mindset and committing to the process is a critical starting point, motivation and clearly defined goals are not all that you need. That is why I created a process for you to follow as you work to improve as a speaker. Let's begin by exploring the first phase in my *Teach the Geek to Speak* process – Pre-Speech.

Pre-Speech

Chapter 3

Shall I refuse my dinner because I do not fully understand the process of digestion?

~ Oliver Heaviside

Identify Your Audience. As I have shared, giving presentations at my job and at conferences was a nightmare for me. Speaking literally made me sick and sweaty.

In my mind, at that time, I felt that speaking publicly about my work was outside of my scope of responsibilities. "I am a STEM guy!" I'd say to myself. "I don't want to talk in front of people. I am an engineer." To make matters worse, I was out of practice at speaking in public. While studying in secondary school, speaking was not required in AP

Chemistry, AP Biology, or any of my other science courses. I was a geek. I did not need to speak!

Nonetheless, as a STEM professional, I learned that to perform my job at the high level I desired, I needed to speak. I needed to speak well and to speak often. I remember the day that my Project Supervisor and Coordinator asked me to keep him and the Executive Team abreast, every month, on the status of the project to which my team and I were assigned. He wanted me to keep them all informed by giving them a monthly presentation that they would use to determine whether we would maintain our assignment.

The day that I had to present seemed to approach very quickly. Sweat was rising from my armpits and I felt like I was hyperventilating. I took myself into a corner and gave myself a pep talk. I was scared. Somehow, I managed to deliver the information on behalf of my team to our Executive Team and did fairly well -- well enough that my superiors and my co-workers began to call on me to be the office's public speaker.

As I accepted the fact that I was going to need to speak for work, I decided that I wanted to become really good at it. I eventually enrolled in online classes, forums, and webinars to learn how to become the caliber of speaker that I wanted to be. I soon realized that I did not need to be afraid and I didn't need to refuse to speak, I only needed a process to help allay my fears and to achieve my goal of effectively engaging my audience. I also wanted to be able to do so without noticeable fear.

As Nadine Smith notes in her article on how to identify your target audience, "Speeches succeed or fail based on your ability to reach your target audience. If your target audience is not interested in your topic or is unable to understand your level of vocabulary, your speech will always fall on deaf ears." Smith stresses the importance of knowing your audience in general and reminds us that being aware of our vocabulary when speaking is the key. This is especially important to us as STEM professionals, since our target audiences are sometimes non-science professionals. There may be situations where you cannot avoid using terms with which your audience may not be familiar. A pre-speech activity that you can do to ensure that your audience understands exactly what you are presenting is to create a glossary of terms that you review and share with them at some point before or during your talk.

This pre-speech step of planning to speak -- identifying your audience -- can be accomplished in several ways. Depending on the nature of your speaking assignment, you should determine the characteristics, demographics, socioeconomic backgrounds, wishes and desires of your audience. When you do not have this information before you address an audience, you will appear to be unprepared and risk failing to accomplish what is needed to deliver an outstanding talk.

The three primary groups of people that you will present to have different needs.

Senior Management

The people who run the company have corner offices, their own administrative assistants, and not much time to spare. You need to ask yourself, "What do they know about my project?" They may not know anything about your area of expertise. In those instances, you have to ask yourself, "What will they want to know?" or "What do I need to teach them in the presentation?" Each manager will have their own interests, based on their specific area of responsibility. The COO will want to know how what you are talking about impacts efficiency. The CFO will want to know how much it will cost the company and how much profit it will generate for the company. The CTO will want to know about innovation and timelines. Each of these managers may make up your audience. How do you meet all their concerns? You should ask them what they want and need you to share with them. If they are not available, ask their administrative assistants what their manager's main concerns are. You should then be sure that you answer their concerns in your presentation.

When your presentations are an efficient use of the managers' time and your speaking meets their needs or helps them to understand your work, you will quickly gain the attention, respect and appreciation of your superiors.

Other Engineers/Fellow STEM Professionals

When your audience is your fellow STEM professionals, you can be more technical. However, you still need to present quickly and efficiently. During a project team meeting, for instance, if you need a certain colleague to perform a task before you can move forward with your task, include that in your presentation and make sure that you also include other important calls to actions in your presentation. Remember to pause during your presentation so that you can ask, while you are presenting, when the co-worker you need to assist the team will complete the assigned task. This helps to ensure that the colleague will be accountable, since they will have to respond to you in front of the entire group.

Non-STEM Audiences

Non-STEM audiences are similar to audiences that may include supervisors or other engineers. These audiences may not know all the technical terms that you use in your profession. However, they still want to know what you are doing and how they can help. For these audiences, you need to introduce terms that are likely foreign to them very early in your talk. Preparing a glossary of terms to distribute before I speak works exceptionally well for this group, too.

Working as an engineer, I worked in the Orthobiologics space. Working in Orthobiologics, I worked with osteoblasts. Very few people who were not in the field would know what an osteoblast is. Therefore, early in my presentation, I would explain to my audience that an osteoblast is a large cell that makes bone. That's all. Could I be much more specific in defining this term? Of course, but there was no need for me to go into more detail with an audience who was unfamiliar with scientific terms. However, my brief definition of the term early in my talk allowed me to use the word throughout my presentation with the confidence that my audience understood exactly what I was saying for the rest of my talk.

I had to prepare frequent conference presentations; perhaps you do, too. If you are not presenting yet, it is a good idea to have started reading this book now. This is because as you climb the corporate ladder to success, you will have to present to your peers and others. Since academic and professional conference audiences have people from a variety of industries with a diversity of expertise, they should be treated like non-STEM audiences. This involves defining your terms early and providing your audiences with a glossary of terms when necessary.

Understand Your Audience

A buffet-style dinner, in my mind, means all you can eat. It was obvious that no one had defined buffet for the organizers of a professional networking event at which I'd presented. The paid networking event was billed as a buffet-style dinner. However, when the time came to eat, the servers were rationing food from trays in such small portions, I was completely confused as to why it was billed as a buffet. This was not an all you can eat affair. In fact, I barely ate at all. I did not even get to enjoy dessert, because by the time I got to the dessert table, the sweet treats were also gone.

Preparing before speaking is critical. While I was prepared with exactly what I was going to share that evening, I went out on a limb and thought it would give the audience a good laugh if I mentioned, what was to me, the elephant in the room: the non-buffet buffet. So, I went off script and made a joke about it at the beginning of my speech. While the servers laughed hysterically at my joke, my audience fell silent. They did not think that pointing out the obvious was funny at all. As you can imagine, my failed attempt at making my audience laugh created an awkward start to my presentation. Nonetheless, my talk ended well. However, that night taught me a valuable lesson as a speaker. If you plan to go off script, it is critical to know your audience before you do so.

Making the time to understand your audience is important.

Establish Outcomes

People do not want to waste their time listening to presentations without knowing that there will be takeaway messages.

You have to provide people with the information they need to make the right decisions, to improve their situations, or to arrive at the solutions they need for the challenge they are facing. There are many times when you have very little time to provide that information. This makes establishing clear outcomes for your audience very important. Not only is establishing outcomes vital, but as author Darlene Price affirms, we only have about sixty seconds to capture our audience's attention. Therefore, we not only have to establish outcomes, we also must capture our audience's attention quickly and communicate our outcomes fast.

In my case, as an engineer, when I presented, the executives listening wanted to know whether my projects should continue, or whether they should die a terrible death. That is why I always kept three questions in mind when preparing my talks. The three questions to answer before you speak are:

1. Who is your audience?
2. How much does your audience know about your topic?
3. What does the audiences want to know once your speech is done?

Another secret to achieving the outcomes you set for your speech is to get them to care about what you are talking about. As John Ford said, "You can speak well if your tongue can deliver the message of your heart."

How do you get your audience to care? You must care.

In my high school English classes, we often engaged in debates where we were assigned a side to argue on a given topic, whether or not we agreed with the position. It is not easy to defend a position that you do not believe in. Nevertheless, you may be presenting to executives, peers, and people who may not understand every detail and technicality of your work. However, they will be helped by hearing and learning from you. This isn't the debate team.

How do you get people to care? You should speak with confidence and passion. It is important to be yourself, be funny, be interesting, be quirky, and be human. You should share facts. However, you should also tell stories that relate to those facts. That is what engages people. It is important to speak from your heart and to let your own personality come out.

Finally, making an outline from the answers that you gather in your pre-speech research is another way to establish and help you meet the outcomes that you set for your presentation. This involves deciphering ahead of time who your audience is, how much they already know about your topic, and what they want to know once your speech is done.

Remember that people do not like to sit through an entire presentation without having a clear takeaway message. As the speaker, it is your job to capture and hold their attention by caring and speaking passionately and confidently. Your audience should be made to feel important. They should be educated enough on your topic that you don't think sitting through the presentation was a waste of time.

Napoleon Hill said, "Great achievement is usually born of great sacrifice, and is never the result of selfishness." Ensuring the success of your talk depends significantly on the effort you put forth in this pre-speech phase.

Create Relevant Points

Have you ever sat through a speech that seemed to go on forever? This usually happens when a presenter has too many points to make or has not logically organized the talk. We often get to the point where we just don't want to listen anymore and we tune out.

When I was an engineer giving project status updates to my Executive Team, I'd have five focus areas every time. The five points were: Tasks that are done, Tasks that are to be done, Issues and proposed solutions, Cost, and Schedule. These five points were more than enough to talk about and they covered exactly what management wanted to know.

The University of Pittsburgh's Speaking in the Discipline Initiative Research explains exactly why my five-point system works. Their researchers share that, "The fewer the main points, the better. Short classroom speeches under 10 minutes should have no more than three main points. For longer speeches, more than five main points ensures that audiences will have trouble following and remembering the speech." The less people have to retain, the more likely they are to listen.

Therefore, stick to five points or less and resist overwhelming your audience with too much data, jargon, and other information. Three to five points is usually all you really have time to share. It is also about all, as the research confirms, that most audiences have the capacity to handle.

Perfect Your Timing

Related to the number of points that you cover in your speech is the critical issue of timing. A speech's duration is very important for maintaining people's attention. I tell my *Teach the Geek to Speak* students that when given a time limit for a speech, make sure that you finish before you hit the time limit. Concise is nice.

When you finish your talk early, you acknowledge that people are busy. Finishing early is a sign of respect for the time of others. When you finish early, you also leave time for questions and answers.

I used to be a member of the Chamber of Commerce in San Diego. I was a member of a business affiliate group in 2017. I'll never forget the first meeting of that group. The meeting leader asked everyone to introduce themselves and to take no longer than thirty seconds. I actually took out my phone to time my introduction. I took twenty-six seconds. Despite knowing that long introductions take time away from the actual meeting, every single person in that room, except for me, took more than thirty seconds.

People do this all the time. I was quite annoyed. Was it that they just did not care about adhering to time?

For some people, the answer is yes. They are self-absorbed and ignore time limits because they feel that what they have to say is more important than respecting the time of others. They just don't care. However, for the majority of people who exceed time limits when asked to speak, I don't think it's because they don't care. In 1657, philosopher and mathematician Blaise Pascal said, "If I had more time I would have written a shorter letter." Pascal speaks to the heart of the challenge and what he discovered is true. Being concise often takes more time, preparation, and strategic thinking than long-windedness. When you use my *Teach the Geek to Speak* process, you are equipped to give introductions and presentations of various lengths of time and to a variety of audiences.

To help presenters effectively manage their time when preparing to speak, I designed the timing worksheet (available in the *Teach the Geek to Speak* Workbook). There are two types of time that you should be aware of when you present – your actual time and your target time.

Your actual time is the amount of time that you have been given to speak. In my business affiliate group introductions example, the actual time was thirty seconds. I knew that I wanted to finish early, so I needed to establish a target time. The target time is the time that you decide to stop speaking. It should always be earlier than the total overall time that you are allotted to speak. The target time, in my business alliance meeting introduction, was 25 seconds. As I shared, my introduction lasted a total of 26 seconds.

Remember that if you exceed the time limit that you were given for your presentation because your audience is asking you questions, that is not your concern. Keep track of your time when you are practicing and do not let the actual time exceed your target time. If you do this, you will master one of the finer details of speaking like a professional – staying within your time limit.

Speech Structure

Meandering is for gorgeous days and long rides or walks, not for speeches. You want your presentation to have real flow because you want your audience to pay attention and benefit from the information that you have to share with them.

Starting a speech with an engaging question is one of my favorite strategies for professional presentations. You might say something like, "Well, we finally found a solution to that pesky product verification issue. What was it?" After asking that question, you can proceed to answer it in your presentation. Your audience will be clear about exactly what they are listening for and excited about hearing the solutions that you propose.

You typically spend considerable time preparing for a presentation. The outcome of your talk can have a significant impact on your career. Therefore, you want to avoid giving talks that lack intention and do not answer your audience's questions or do not meet their needs.

Another word of caution is to be careful not to muddle the middle. You want to start strong, but you also want to maintain the interest and the structure of your presentation in the middle of your talk. The middle of a speech is where we typically lose people with jargon and unnecessary repetition. One of the best strategies for making sure that your speech remains strong in the middle is to use my five-point maximum technique and make sure that all of your points are easily identifiable.

When it comes to the end of your speech, refer back to something you said at the speech's beginning. Comedians do this all the time. It's referred to as a callback. For example, if you used an opening question like the one I mentioned earlier, then have your last sentence be, "The team and I have been diligent in ferreting out solutions for the product verification issue. We will continue to be diligent." This is your callback. It ties a gorgeous bow on your entire presentation.

Finally, order your speech's points on your *Teach the Geek to Speak* Speech Structure Worksheet (available in the Workbook). This tool helps you to organize your presentation and to be sure that you say everything that you want and need to say in the beginning, middle, and closing of your speech.

PowerPoint Preparation

Imagine that you just finished your slide presentation for a conference. Upon reviewing it, you realize that you have a ton of text on every slide. Do not proceed and do not collect one hundred dollars!

PowerPoint presentations are not dissertations.

You do not want your audience to just read your slides and not be able to focus on what you have to say. If your audience could simply read what you need to communicate, then you could have just sent them an email, article or report.

Think about where we began in our quest to become geeks who speak effectively. We began with mindset. We discussed the necessity of professional development, reading more often, holding ourselves and our colleagues accountable through presenting, understanding our audiences, informing upper management, our peers and the public about our projects and findings, and presenting like we care. Why? Because, even with technology -- email, texts, webinars, and the like -- at times, there is still an inarguable need for us to connect and to communicate voice to voice and face to face with the people we work with, even if virtually, to get our work done well.

Death by PowerPoint does not have to be a thing anymore. Why did it become a thing in the first place? Oftentimes, unprepared or outright terrified speakers use their slides as a crutch to lean on when presenting. When speakers rushed to compile their talks the night before the presentation, and if a presenter did prepare but does not know the content well enough to speak from bullet points alone, they may fill slides with text that they can simply read from. This leads to a non-interactive, boring presentation that makes your audience want to stab themselves, or you, with their pencils.

Besides wanting to avoid the chance of anyone getting injured, there is a biological reason to limit the number of words on your presentation slides. It is called cognitive load. Cognitive load is the capacity of the brain's memory to hold and process new information. Since everyone's capacity to translate information differs, clearly not everyone will be as distracted by a lot of words as others.

However, as a rule, the more words you show your audience, the higher the cognitive load. It follows that the higher the cognitive load, the less information they will be able to retain.

You worked hard to become an expert in your field. Hopefully, you also put effort into preparing your presentation. You want and need your audience to be engaged, to learn, and be able to take the action you want them to take based upon what you have to share. You can ensure that you don't kill people with your PowerPoint presentation by following three simple rules that you can start to use right away.

First, limit the amount of text that you place on each slide to five lines per slide.

Second, use pictures instead of text. When you use pictures, make sure that you select images that are relevant to the words on the screen or relevant to what you are saying when you get to that slide. You should also choose high-quality artwork and be careful to position the images well on your slides. I remember using a photo of myself skydiving in one of my presentations and my audience loved it. Using the image immediately surprised and disarmed my audience. The image showed them that I was adventurous and liked to have fun, it related to my topic, and it persuaded them to give me their full attention during my talk.

The third thing to remember when preparing your presentation is to make sure that the text can be easily read on the background that you choose. If it is not readable, it will be ignored. I prefer to use a white background and black text. If your company requires a certain PowerPoint template, just be careful to place your text in a way that it can be read without straining the audience's vision in any way. If the template is too busy, you can place a white text box on top of the busy slides and type your copy into the text box to ensure that your slides can be easily read. This way, the company template is still used, but solely as a backdrop to the words that you want your audience to be able to focus on and read. When backgrounds are very dark, change your text to white instead of black so that it can be seen more easily.

Finally, to assist you with preparing engaging and effective PowerPoint slides, refer to the *Teach the Geek to Speak* PowerPoint example, which models what your slides could look like. It doubles as a motivational and instructional training and comes with three exercises that you can complete right away so you can be prepared to give an impactful speech when your team or manager calls on you.

Call to Action

Have you ever heard of a call to action? A call to action takes place at the close of a presentation. It is a word, prompt, or instruction that tells the audience to take certain actions.

The call to action makes it clear what actions you want your listeners to take after you speak. While making the call to action is one of the most important parts of presenting, it is also one of the most forgotten aspects in the anatomy of the speech.

You prepared to speak and will deliver your speech for very specific reasons. You made the time to clarify and write down the outcomes and structure of your talk so that you could give an effective presentation. Now, before you end your speech, make certain that you make a clear, concise call to action.

What actions do you want your audience to take post-speech? There is something that you need or want your audience to do so that what you discussed in your presentation can happen. Do not assume that your audience will know what the next step should be. Tell them. For example, if you are presenting to your managers and your team needs particular resources to continue with the project, ask for what you need before you close your presentation.

Have you noticed any calls to action so far in this book? Use the three *Teach the Geek to Speak* worksheets that have been prepared for your pre-speech and during speech phases: The Understanding your Audience Worksheet, The Timing Worksheet and The Speech Structure Worksheet (all available in the *Teach the Geek to Speak* Workbook) are all a part of the beginning of this series to help you prepare for and deliver an excellent and effective presentation.

There's your call to action! Now let's explore the final steps in the *Teach the Geek to Speak* process.

During Speech

Chapter 4

I seem to have been only like a boy playing on the seashore and diverting myself now and then finding a smoother pebble or a prettier shell than ordinary, whilst the great ocean of truth lay all undiscovered before me.

~ Isaac Newton

You now have a clear understanding of how important developing the proper mindset and being consistent in personal development are to transform you into an effective speaker. You have also learned and practiced the initial phase of The *Teach the Geek to Speak* process -- Pre-Speech.

The second phase of the process is During Speech. Here we review seven key factors that, once mastered, will assist you in becoming a more confident, more polished, and more effective public speaker.

Gestures

Most of the professionals (including me) in my field tend to be logical in our thinking. If you are a STEM professional, you are also probably very logical. One result of this trait is that we often tend to think more about the message that we want to convey and the facts that need to be stated than we do about more abstract factors, such as hand movements, moving around the room, varying the sound of our voice, eye contact, and the various other non-verbal components of giving an effective presentation.

What do you do with your hands when you are speaking? How should you move about the room? Should you gesture? Is any of this important at all?

A gesture is any movement of any part of your body, especially your hands and your head, to express ideas and meaning. The topic of gestures is frequently discussed when studying public speaking. As a matter of fact, researchers have published some helpful and fascinating facts about how to use gestures to make your presentations more effective.

Co-speech and emblem gestures are the two main categories of gestures. Co-speech gestures correspond with what you say. These gestures are used to help your audience better comprehend the points you want to convey. They are used in tandem with spoken words. On the other hand, emblem gestures are used to communicate a thought or feeling without using spoken words.

There are four types of co-speech gestures: Iconic gestures, Deictic or Pointing Gestures, Metaphoric Gestures, and Beat Gestures.

Iconic gesturing is the use of hand motions to describe an object, individual physical attributes, or actions, or to describe spatial relationships. For example, you may use your hands to show that someone is petite in stature, that you were wandering down a long road, or to show the dimensions and shape of the product you are developing.

Did your mother ever tell you it was impolite to point? When it comes to gesturing as a speaker, mom's rules about pointing do not apply. Deictic gestures are the second type of co-speech gesturing. It describes the use of pointing, usually with your index finger extended, to the person, place, thing or idea that you want your audience to pay close attention to. In your speech, you may use deictic gestures to highlight key points on your PowerPoint or to draw your audience's attention to props or charts that you are using from the stage.

Third, using metaphoric gestures can be an impactful way to communicate with your audience. Metaphoric gestures help us to show more abstract ideas such as love, peace, or hope. These are all abstract ideas that we can show with our hands or by asking the audience to show by using their hands. If you want to make a statement about love for example, you may form a heart with your fingers and place it on your chest.

Finally, beat gestures have no semantic meaning, but simply help the speaker keep time or add emphasis during a speech. Beat gestures have no semantic meaning, but emblem gestures do. Emblems are used to indicate meaning without talking at all. Therefore, to communicate hope, you may hold your hand up for the audience to see and then cross your fingers, and you could hold up your index and middle fingers at the same time and your audience would automatically know that you are saying peace or goodbye.

It is worth noting in our discussion about gestures that we live in a global society. Consequently, as you become a more skilled presenter, depending on where your company does business, you will interact with different cultures. Be careful that you are culturally conscious. When you use gestures, be positive that you do not use gestures that may offend the people you are there to win over with your talk.

As we all know, standing before an audience can be intimidating. Nonetheless, remaining composed during your speech is crucial. If your gestures feel forced, they will appear disingenuous to your audience. Don't use them in your presentation. Gestures that are over done or that seem unnatural could ruin or severely lessen the effect of your presentation.

A strategy I use to keep myself calm and composed when I have to speak is to associate speaking and keeping my audience engaged to having a personal discussion with one of my colleagues or peers. Connecting my experience of being on stage to something that I do naturally every day -- talk to my friends -- helps me to become more conscious of how I talk and how I express myself from the stage.

Gestures are like icing on the cake. You can eat cake without icing, but the cake is usually much more delicious with the icing. Similarly, the words that you actually use in your speech are the cake. The words that you use when speaking matter most, but when you skillfully use gestures, these gestures decorate or enhance your presentation. They make our talk much more effective and enjoyable for the audience. Therefore, start practicing using the four types of co-speech gestures that you learned in this section. The next time you present, use what you learned about gestures to help you to clearly and concisely convey your message.

It is important for me to note that in many mainstream training courses or groups, there is an overemphasis on non-verbal communication during a presentation. That overemphasis was a major factor that contributed to the creation of the *Teach the Geek to Speak* process. Giving an effective presentation as STEM professionals simply does not necessitate some of what other talks require to be effective.

I once served as one of the evaluators for a talk that one of my peers was giving in our speaking club. I vividly recall how frustrated I was at my fellow evaluator's feedback to the presenter. Neither of them evaluated the presenter on the content, quality, flow or organization of the talk. They did not seem to notice whether the presenter accomplished the goal as a presenter. They focused on things such as the speaker patting her leg while she spoke, and on the fact that she had not moved about the room during her presentation. In certain types of presentations, those types of things may make or break a speaker's presentation success. That may not be the case in STEM presentations, which is another reason why I saw such a need for this book. Standing in front of a lectern works just fine, and is often the setup for many technical presentations.

Regardless of how well you begin to incorporate the use of gestures into your presentations, remember that the quality of your content and what you say reign supreme. Perfect gesturcs will never make up for an ill-prepared or poorly rendered speech.

Establish Eye Contact

It has been said that the eyes are the windows to the soul. I used to struggle with making eye contact with my audience, but I was able to overcome that discomfort by using the following techniques.

Regardless of the topic on which you are speaking or the industry that you are an expert in, the main goal of presenting is to inform and persuade your audience. Maintaining eye contact as a public speaker may make you uncomfortable, but it is vital for you to connect, eye to eye, with the people to whom you are presenting. Making eye contact builds connection and trust. You have to look at your audience if you want the audience to look at you.

According to research conducted at Cornell University, researchers measured how consumers bought Trix cereal based on if the character on the box was illustrated to look directly at the customer or if the character was looking away from the customer. It was interesting that researchers discovered consumers bought more Trix cereal when the rabbit on the box looked directly at them instead of looking away from them. When the company made sure that the image on their cereal boxes made eye contact with the prospective buyers (which may have seemed like an insignificant adjustment), it resulted in a significant increase in the sales of Trix cereal.

As public speakers or as individuals who aspire to speak, we can learn a lot about how powerful eye contact is from this research.

One trick that speakers can use to increase audience interest and engagement and to get their audiences to buy into what they are sharing is the three second rule. This rule initiates and increases eye contact with the audience. The strategy is simply to intentionally lock eyes with each audience member, or to at least give the impression that you are locking eyes with them, for at least three seconds during your speech. Although three seconds of eye contact is not a lot of time, it is something to aim for. This is because the benefits of achieving eye contact with your audience are significant.

In the early phase of my quest to become a better presenter, a mentor of mine said that my eye contact needed to improve. He suggested that I look people in my audience in the eye for at least three seconds each. I was new to the group we belonged to and eager to learn and improve. Therefore, as soon as I had the opportunity to speak again, I tried it and I immediately knew that it would not be a sustainable technique for me. Staring at one person in the eyes for three second felt awkward. While using the three-second technique may have improved my eye contact, it also caused me to become extremely distracted overall. As a matter of fact, I was so distracted that I would constantly forget the next point that I was supposed to make. This led me to create another strategy you can use: look at people's eyebrows instead of directly into their eyes.

Usually, there is enough distance between you and your audience that if you concentrate on the audience members' eyebrows, you ease the discomfort of direct eye contact. However, you give the appearance of looking into their eyes. Looking into an audience member's eyebrows is less distracting and intimidating than looking into their eyes. Using this *Teach the Geek to Speak* technique enables you to still reap the benefits that come with connecting with your audience eye to eye until you sharpen your skills and confidence to be able to do so without forgetting what you want to say next.

Keep in mind that it is okay to look away from your audience's eyes or eyebrows every so often. As a matter of fact, it is necessary. You may need to look away so that you do not draw a blank and to maintain the flow of your talk. Just remember once you reset yourself for the next part of your talk to reconnect -- eye to eye or eyebrow to eyebrow – with your audience.

Voice Volume, Speed and Breathing

Quantified Impressions, a communications company asserts, "The sound of a speaker's voice matters twice as much as the content of the message."

When it comes to the topic of voice in public speaking, there is a lot of ground that we can cover. However, I have found that it makes the most sense to focus first on these two key areas: tone and pace.

Tone

Researchers at San Diego State University and Columbia Business School affirm that listeners often associate voices that are higher in volume with authority. In essence, we listen more intently and are more trusting of speakers when we can hear them loudly and clearly. This is why I coach *Teach the Geek to Speak* clients to be positive that your audience can hear you. If you are working with a microphone, and especially when you are not, if you are not sure that you can be heard loudly and clearly, then you should pause before jumping into your talk to ask your audience if they can hear you.

You must project your voice to make sure that everyone hears what you are saying. This is especially important when you are speaking to an audience that may speak a different language. You have to be aware that you may have to adjust your tone so they understand your accent.

Pace

Speaking speed matters. The brains of your listeners only work so fast and public speaking is already challenging. Therefore, mastering how to pace yourself is critical to ensuring that you have an effective presentation.

At what pace should you be speaking? This depends on the nature of the audience to whom you are presenting. Whenever possible, learn ahead of time who will be in the room when you are speaking.

If you are addressing a welcoming audience, speak more slowly (around 140 words per minute) so that your audience can truly enjoy what you are saying. When you speak to a hostile audience, speak more quickly. This gives your audience less of a chance to refute or dismiss your message. In those instances, monitor your pace and speak at about 160 words per minute. When you are giving a technical talk, you should opt for a slower speed of 110 to 140 words per minute so your audience has time to listen to and process the new and unfamiliar information that you are sharing with them.

Audience members focus their attention on your tone and pace. However, they also pay attention to how confident and composed you appear to be when you are presenting. Consequently, knowing how to breath is a third and essential skill to develop as you work to improve your presentation skills.

Sometimes during a talk, you can begin to feel breathless. However, during your presentation is no time to lose your breath. You have done a lot to pre-pare for your talk, so when the moment comes to showcase your efforts -- no shallow breaths are allowed.

To relax yourself, take deep, cleansing breaths from your diaphragm at least three times before you begin to speak. When you begin to speak from the front of the room, breathe from your diaphragm. Breathing properly during your presentation not only helps to calm and settle you, it helps your voice quality, helps you to pace yourself, and improves your posture. This sets you up to make a stellar presentation.

PowerPoint Use

In our earlier discussion on PowerPoint preparation, I gave you guidance on how to compose an effective slide deck that included several steps to ensure that your audience does not fall prey to death by PowerPoint at your hands. However, preparing an effective PowerPoint is just step one in the process. You also have to present the information on your slides with enough skill and enthusiasm to ensure that you communicate your message, inform your audience, make your call to action, and keep your audience engaged throughout. This is when my *Teach the Geek to Speak* Cardinal Rules of PowerPoint Use come into to play.

While there are a number of tips that I could give you, I only have two cardinal rules:

1. Make sure that your body is facing the audience
2. Do not read from your slides

Make sure that your body faces your audience. Even when you need to refer to information on your slide, glance or point at what you want to bring their attention to. However, do not turn your entire body away from your audience. When you turn from the audience or read from your slides, you lose eye contact with them. You do not want to forfeit the trust that listeners grant you when you face and look at them. As we discussed when we reviewed the research about the Trix rabbit on the cereal box, eye contact is directly related to your likelihood of "selling" or moving your audience to take the action you want them to take. Remember, your slides should have minimal text, so there should not be a lot for you to read.

While preparing and then presenting your slides with confidence and clarity can make your presentation unforgettable, failing to prepare and present your slides effectively can ruin your efforts. The important thing is to face your audience when you are speaking and to not read from your slides. Your PowerPoint should serve as a powerful support for your message and as a tool that helps you to win your audience over and make them eager to respond to your call of action.

Take Excellent Notes

I feel pretty strongly about how we use notes during a presentation. Do you tend to write out your entire speech and then read the whole thing when you present?

Although a public speaker may rely on their notes when practicing in the mirror at home, they should not depend on their notes during the actual presentation. Therefore, if you are reading from notes during all your presentations . . . STOP!

The purpose of note cards is for you to have statistics, important quotes, presentation-related data and other detailed, difficult to remember information at your fingertips. However, when you are trained to present effectively, are properly prepared, and are passionate and knowledgeable about your topic, you do not need to read directly from note cards.

Michael Hines, professor at Hankuk University of Foreign Studies (in Korea), conducted research to learn which modes of notetaking were most effective for public speakers. The results of his study suggest that when bullet points within notes are practiced and used during the speech, a public speaker's ability and skill increase exponentially. Professor Hines lectured on a topic for 60 minutes and then gave his study participants ten minutes to formulate a speech. He randomly picked participants to give a three-minute speech on the topic without using detailed notes. He measured each participants' level of comfort and ability with public speaking before and after the study. He found that there was a statistically significant increase in the participants' public speaking ability.

How to Remember Your Speech

You are probably thinking, "Neil! I am already very uncomfortable with public speaking. You now want to take my notes away! You're a madman."

I assure you that making you more at ease before your audience is my goal. Don't worry, my methods work!

Let's walk through the process of how to make and review your notes in a way that will have you prepared, equipped and confident about your next presentation.

First, do not assume that you do not need to practice your presentation. Even if you are an expert on the content that you are presenting, or if you have given the presentation more than once -- practice. Think about what you want to say, how you want to say it, and what you need to accomplish once your speech is finished. When you prepare by practicing, you always deliver a more confident, more polished, and more effective talk.

Now that we have established that practicing before you speak is a non-negotiable, when you practice your speech, you need to make a list of topics. What are the three to five main topics that you have to cover in order for your talk to be successful? Write them down.

After you establish the three to five major topics that you need to cover and write them down, you are ready for the next step in this process which is to list under each topic up to three points that you need to address that are directly related to that topic.

Finally, you need to memorize all of your topics and all of the related bullet points beneath each of those topics. Because you are the expert, you know the information. You know the details that correspond to each topic and to each bullet point under those topics, so you will simply study the main topics and points and speak, based on your knowledge, from that outline. If you do not know the content, part of preparing to speak is for you to study the information to the degree that you can speak about each topic and its related points without detailed notes in your hand. This will save your audience from listening to you read instead of present. It will also save you from appearing ill-equipped and unprofessional during your talk. Adequate practice will increase your confidence, ensure that you sound natural while presenting the information you have to share and will still provide the security you need just in case you lose your place or become distracted while you are presenting.

Without the notes, you appear more knowledgeable and you have more of an opportunity to look at the audience, even if you really are just looking at their eyebrows.

Track your Fillers

Conciseness and clarity are two marks of an experienced public speaker. Few things diminish one's ability to be concise and clear like using fillers does.

Fillers or nonsense words are words like, "so," "um," "ya know," "like," and "oh". You may slip up and use fillers occasionally in your presentations. However, when these words are overused, they can distract your listeners, de-edify you as the expert, and weaken your overall message.

There is no hard and fast rule whether you should totally eliminate using fillers when you present. Some research links filler words with greater conscientiousness, listener recall, and listener comprehension.

For example, despite his use of fillers when he speaks, former President of the United States of America, President Barack Obama, is considered to be an exceptional public speaker. Let's be clear that our former president is an exception to the rule when it comes to being able to navigate a general rule of speaking and still capture the hearts and minds of an audience. For this reason, I recommend that you avoid using filler words as much as possible when you present.

As a matter of fact, this is precisely why I created a tool to help you identify and limit the number of fillers that you use when you speak. It is the fourth stage in the *Teach the*

Geek to Speak process. It is called the Filler Word Tracker, and it's in the *Teach the Geek to Speak* Workbook. This tool is used in conjunction with recording your speeches to help you assess and hone your skills. This will allow you to speak purposefully and remain focused during your presentations so you get the intended response from your audience.

It is not uncommon to feel rushed to move on to your next point and to answer quickly when you are asked a question. You need to relax. Take your time and do not waste words. Many of the words that you use to fill the empty space when you speak can be eliminated if you are deliberate about taking your time while presenting.

"Pause, think, answer" is a speaking strategy that you can use to slow down your mind and body when you present. Slowing down instantly helps you to avoid saying extra words just to fill the space and time.

To use this technique effectively, however, you have to become comfortable with silence. Silence between thoughts helps you to convey your next idea with clarity and reduces your tendency to use fillers.

Post-Speech

Chapter 5

One, remember to look up at the stars and not down at your feet. Two, never give up work. Work gives you meaning, and purpose and life is empty without it. Three, if you are lucky enough to find love, remember it is there and don't throw it away.

~ Stephen Hawking

Get Feedback. You have prepared and delivered your speech. So you think you are done, right? Wrong. Practicing and presenting are a given.

However, acquiring feedback from your audience is just as important when you are serious about improving so you can meet your goals.

Feedback is essential to your general personal and professional development and is important for you as a public speaker. While people may offer you unsolicited feedback, I highly recommend that you ask people for their feedback. As a matter of fact, as a STEM professional, you should seek constructive criticism from your colleagues.

It makes sense to ask for feedback after your presentation. However, asking for feedback does not just have to occur after your talk. You put considerable time and effort into preparing. Since practice is non-negotiable, you make time, as we discussed in the previous chapter, to practice your presentation before you hit the stage. Therefore, why not ask people you trust to critique your talk before you speak? When they offer you their feedback, you can adjust your presentation as needed and go into your talk already having benefitted from the insights of others. You should seek feedback before your presentation. Just be sure to ask for feedback from people that you trust.

Although I am an advocate of soliciting feedback, if you do not agree with the feedback – don't take it. Do not feel compelled to implement every suggestion that you receive. Think of the surveys or evaluations that you will collect as a buffet. You never eat every single thing that is available there. You pick and choose what you want to eat. Like Forrest said in the movie Forrest Gump, "Life is like a box of chocolates and you never know what you're going to get." The same goes for feedback. Listen to all feedback. Implement what makes sense.

On the day of your presentation, you can let your audience know before you start speaking that you value their insights and that you want their feedback at the close of your talk. You can use the questionnaire that I have designed for you. It is the fifth step in the *Teach the Geek to Speak* process and in the Workbook. You can edit that document as needed to help you get the information you need from your audience so you can improve as a speaker.

Feedback is critical to the process of perfecting your skill as a public speaker.

Conduct a Personal Inventory

Personal inventory, or what I call looking inward, is one of the best ways to become a more effective public speaker. When I say personal inventory, I am truly encouraging you to take and watch video of yourself giving your talks. It can be painful to watch, but whenever possible, have your speeches recorded and watch the videos afterwards.

When your speeches are recorded, you have the opportunity to analyze and make corrections to your presentations based on what you see.

During your personal inventory, by way of watching the recording of your speech, write down your questions as if you are an audience member who is listening to your presentation. Pay close attention to the areas that you wanted to work on. For example, are you working on eye contact or on limiting your fillers? Watch for these gestures and listen to your tone and flow as you speak. Take note of the areas in which you have improved and where you still need to practice.

As an added bonus, when your speech is recorded, you can also examine other important aspects of public speaking. You can observe whether your audience is engaged, looking at you, smiling and laughing, having side conversations with one another, or using their phones. These are all elements that contribute to you giving an effective presentation. They can all be measured well when you watch recordings of your talks.

As you critique your work as a public speaker, your personal inventory should serve as honest, detailed feedback from which you begin to adjust. As you work on your personal inventory, remember to use the resources from this sixth and final step in the *Teach the Geek to Speak* process. Look for your Personal Inventory worksheet (in the Workbook) and compare and contrast that worksheet with your Speech Structure worksheet. Together, these two resources will help you to determine whether you covered all the points you needed to cover, made a call to action, and more.

Teach the Geek to Speak

Six Step Process for STEM Professionals to Achieve Speaking Success

STEM professionals are used to following a process. We operate according to protocols, standard operating procedures, and work instructions. As a product development engineer in the medical devices industry, I followed a process to develop a product. The government required it!

I have also developed a six-step process, specifically for people in STEM professions, which helps you to prepare and deliver any speech. This includes a presentation at work, a conference talk, or even a eulogy!

The first step is audience analysis. A presenter must tailor their speech to those in the audience. Presenters often skip this step. Being mindful of the people in the audience helps you to decide what should be in the presentation.

The second step is timing. A respectful presenter will always tailor their speech to be within the time limit. A speech that goes over time is a hallmark of poor preparation.

The third step is speech structure. Coming up with your opening, the points you want to cover, and a memorable closing are all critical in delivering a speech. In addition to being mindful of timing, you'll use this speech structure when you're practicing your speech.

The fourth step is the questionnaire. Getting feedback as a presenter is key to getting better. You'll prepare a series of questions to ask audience members to get critical feedback.

The fifth step is fillers. Um, ah, you know -- the types of words that pepper our everyday casual conversations also creep into our professional presentations. To minimize fillers, you must become aware that you are using them and how often.

The sixth and final step is personal inventory. To truly become a better public speaker, it's important that you look at video of yourself presenting. This helps you to identify your filler words and their frequency. It also helps you to see how closely the speech you gave mirrored the speech you practiced using your speech structure.

Of course, some of the steps won't apply, depending on the situation. You're likely not going to provide a questionnaire to people at a eulogy. However, this is the six-step *Teach the Geek to Speak* process.

It's comprehensive and efficient -- just the way we STEM professionals like it! You know what else is comprehensive and efficient? The *Teach the Geek to Speak* workbook, a resource where you can find worksheets that cover this six-step process.

Afterword

It is no secret that most people would rather be in the coffin than give the eulogy. As a matter of fact, a number of statistics affirm that public speaking is noted as people's number one fear next to death.

Becoming an effective public speaker can seem complicated at first, just like any new and exciting endeavor. However, it is worth exploring. The *Teach the Geek to Speak* process gives you all the things a public speaker must remember and do to get excellent results. Implement the process, use the resource tools in the Workbook, and visualize yourself giving the presentation that you need to give to meet your professional and personal goals. You know what? You will!

Teach the Geek to Speak is a process that equips novice and intermediate presenters to quickly improve. As a STEM professional, it serves no purpose to remain silent in a cubicle, unless that is what you choose to do. Public speakers with our expertise are in demand globally. You can travel throughout the world speaking and teaching others in your area of expertise and making a significant difference for your company, as well as for yourself and others. Take what you have learned in *Teach the Geek to Speak* process to conduct seminars, webinars, podcasts, presentations, and speeches at various STEM related meetings, conferences, and other settings.

Mr. Les Brown, one of the world's most renowned speakers, a man who graces the Speaker's Hall of Fame, says it best, "Once you open your mouth, you tell the world who you are."

Congratulations on making the investment in yourself to perfect your skills as a public speaker in the STEM professions. Go, open your mouth, and confidently tell others about the areas of your field of expertise that matter most to you. The sky is the limit for you!

Public speaking is someone else's job, until it's yours. Well, guess what? It's yours, and with The Teach the Geek to Speak process, you can speak with skill and confidence. Have fun!

~ Neil Thompson

About the Author

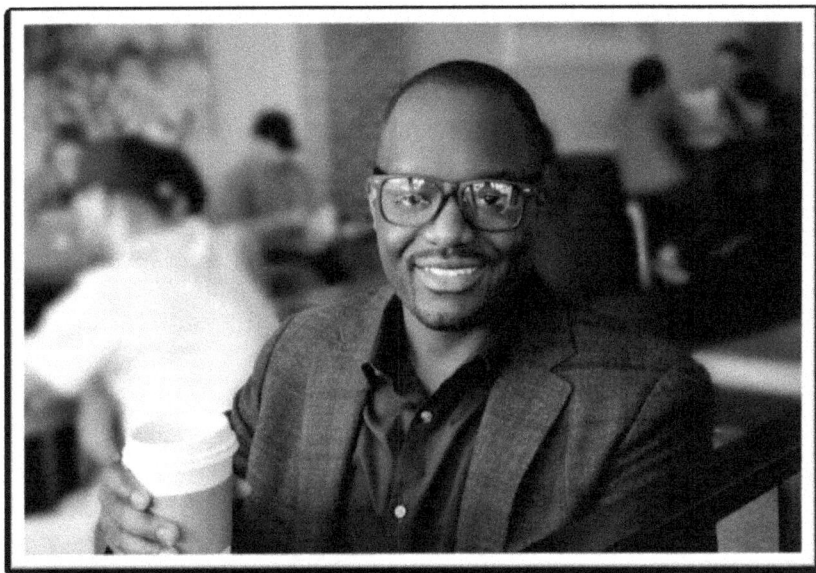

Neil Thompson is a speaker, writer and founder of Teach the Geek, an online platform for STEM professionals. A former product development engineer, Neil has been published in the *San Diego Business Journal*, *Mechanical Engineering Magazine*, *Tech Directions Magazine*, and *PsychCentral*. He is a member of the San Diego Entrepreneurs Ex-change, San Diego Entrepreneurs Group and Speakers Guild USA.

To learn more about Neil visit: **teachthegeek.com**

www.ingramcontent.com/pod-product-compliance
Lightning Source LLC
Chambersburg PA
CBHW071115210326
41519CB00020B/6303